Jumpstarters for Root Words, Prefixes, and Suffixes

Short Daily Warm-ups for the Classroom

By
CINDY BARDEN

COPYRIGHT © 2008 Mark Twain Media, Inc.

ISBN 978-1-58037-438-5

Printing No. CD-404081

Mark Twain Media, Inc., Publishers
Distributed by Carson-Dellosa Publishing Company, Inc.

Table of Contents

Introduction to the Teacher

Physical warm-ups help athletes prepare for more strenuous types of activity. Mental warm-ups help students prepare for the day's lesson while reviewing what they have previously learned.

The short warm-up activities presented in this book provide teachers and parents with a variety of ways for students to practice and reinforce the skills they have already learned. Each page contains five warm-ups—one for each day of the week. Used at the beginning of class, warm-ups help students focus on a specific topic.

Learning the meaning of prefixes and suffixes helps students increase their vocabulary and enables them to become better communicators. The warm-up activities in this book cover the meaning of commonly used prefixes and suffixes, help students improve dictionary and vocabulary skills, and provide practice in sentence writing and critical thinking. Students also have opportunities to make deductions, write synonyms and antonyms, and determine the meaning of words from context.

A list of words with prefixes and suffixes is included at the end of the book for reference and can be used with students for review, vocabulary, or spelling.

Encourage students to get into the "look it up" habit by using a dictionary when they are unsure of the meaning or spelling of a word.

Suggestions for use:

- Copy and cut apart one page each week. Give students one warm-up activity each day at the beginning of class.
- Give each student a copy of the entire page to complete day by day. Students can keep the completed pages in a three-ring binder to use as a resource.
- Make transparencies of individual warm-ups and complete the activities as a group.
- Provide extra copies of warm-ups in your learning center for students to complete at random when they have a few extra minutes.
- Keep some warm-ups on hand to use as fill-ins when the class has a few extra minutes before lunch or dismissal.

Root Word, Prefix, & Suffix Warm-ups: Root Words, Prefixes, & Suffixes

Name/Date _____

Note: Some root words have foreign origins, often Latin or Greek. For example, *inhale* and *exhale* are words with prefixes, even though the root word *hale* isn't a common English word.

Root Words, Prefixes, & Suffixes 1

1. A root word is a word that can be changed into a new word by adding a prefix and/or suffix to it. *Like* is a root word. Write two other examples of root words. _____

2. A prefix is added to the beginning of a word and changes its meaning. (*dislike*) Write two more examples. _____

3. A suffix is added to the end of a word and changes its meaning. (*likely*) Write two more examples. _____

4. Some words can contain both a prefix and a suffix. (*unlikely*) Write two more examples. _____

UN- DIS- RE- -FUL -LESS -ABLE -NESS

Name/Date _____

Root Words, Prefixes, & Suffixes 2

1. The spelling of root words usually does not change when prefixes are added. Example: *resell*. Write two more examples.

   _____

2. In the words *real, really,* and *read,* the *re-* at the beginning of the words is not a prefix. Why not? _____

   _____

Name/Date _____

Root Words, Prefixes, & Suffixes 3

Write the root words.

1. unthinkable   2. illegal

   _____   _____

3. honesty   4. mismanagement

   _____   _____

5. impossible   6. disconnection

   _____   _____

Name/Date _____

Root Words, Prefixes, & Suffixes 4

Add a prefix, suffix, or both to each root word. Write the new words.

1. luck   2. quick

   _____   _____

3. sleep   4. reach

   _____   _____

5. pay   6. read

   _____   _____

Name/Date _____

Root Words, Prefixes, & Suffixes 5

Explain the difference between compound words, such as *lighthouse*, and words with prefixes and suffixes.

_____

_____

_____

_____

Root Word, Prefix, & Suffix Warm-ups: Root Words, Prefixes, & Suffixes

---

Name/Date _____

Root Words, Prefixes, & Suffixes 6

Sometimes the spelling of a root word changes when a suffix is added. Write the root words. Check a dictionary if you are not sure of the spelling.

1. unbelievable   2. unhappily
   _____   _____

3. reappearance   4. unfriendly
   _____   _____

5. rechargeable   6. disagreement
   _____   _____

Name/Date _____

Root Words, Prefixes, & Suffixes 7

Consider words like *repaint, rethink,* and *redo.* What do you think the prefix *re-* means?

_____

_____

_____

Name/Date _____

Root Words, Prefixes, & Suffixes 8

Add the prefix *re-* to each word and use it in a short sentence.

1. move   _____

2. pay   _____

3. place _____

4. set   _____

5. try   _____

Name/Date _____

Root Words, Prefixes, & Suffixes 9

Add *re-* to each word. On your own paper, write a short definition of each new word that does not include the word *again. Example:* assemble: reassemble—to put back together

1. appoint   2. connect   3. decorate
   _____   _____   _____

4. check   5. style
   _____   _____

Name/Date _____

Root Words, Prefixes, & Suffixes 10

List 10 or more words that begin with the prefix *re-*. Circle the root words.

_____

_____

_____

_____

_____

Root Word, Prefix, & Suffix Warm-ups: Prefixes With Negative Meanings

---

Name/Date _____

Prefixes With Negative Meanings 1

Circle the prefix in each word. Underline the root words.

1. unlike
2. illogic
3. inappropriate
4. inconsiderate
5. nonprofit
6. disappear
7. disadvantage
8. nonsense
9. improbable
10. impossible

Name/Date _____

Prefixes With Negative Meanings 2

Consider the meaning of these words: unlike, illogic, inappropriate, inconsiderate, disappear, disadvantage, nonprofit, nonsense, improbable, and impossible.

What do the prefixes *un-, il-, in-, im-, non-,* and *dis-* have in common?

_____

_____

_____

Name/Date _____

Prefixes With Negative Meanings 3

Add the prefix *un-* to the root words given. Write the new word. On your own paper, write a short definition for each word that doesn't include the word *not. Example:* un + happy = unhappy: sad

1. able   2. like   3. do
   _____   _____   _____

4. made   5. cover
   _____   _____

Name/Date _____

Prefixes With Negative Meanings 4

Write 10 words that begin with the prefix *un-*. Circle the root words.

UN=NOT

_____

_____

_____

_____

Name/Date _____

Prefixes With Negative Meanings 5

Write words from the list to match the definitions. Keep in mind the meaning of the prefix and the root words.

disable	disarm	discharge	discolored
disloyal	disorder	disrespect	disrepair

_____ 1. falling apart   _____ 2. make harmless

_____ 3. chaos   _____ 4. false

_____ 5. make useless   _____ 6. stained

_____ 7. release from duty   _____ 8. rudeness

4

Root Word, Prefix, & Suffix Warm-ups: Prefixes With Negative Meanings

---

Name/Date _____

Prefixes With Negative Meanings 6

1. How can knowing the meaning of a prefix and the root word help you understand the meaning of a new word?

   _____

   _____

2. If you know the meaning of the prefix, but not the root word, how can that help you understand the meaning of the new word?

   _____

   _____

Name/Date _____

Prefixes With Negative Meanings 7

Add the prefix *un-* or *dis-* to each word. Write the new words.

1. trust

   _____

2. agree

   _____

3. true

   _____

4. place

   _____

5. obey

   _____

6. bearable

   _____

Name/Date _____

Prefixes With Negative Meanings 8

The prefixes *dis-, in-, il-, im-, non-,* and *un-* change a word so that it means the opposite. On your own paper, write definitions for the underlined words without using the word *not*.

1. *Finite* means limited. What does *infinite* mean?

2. *Appropriate* means right or correct. What does *inappropriate* mean?

3. *Patient* means calm and accepting. What does *impatient* mean?

4. A *dispensable* item is one that is not needed. What does *indispensable* mean?

5. *Logical* means reasonable. What does *illogical* mean?

Name/Date _____

Prefixes With Negative Meanings 9

Circle 16 words that begin with *un-* in the puzzle. List the words on another sheet of paper.

L	N	U	L	U	U	D	E	S	U	N	U
A	W	U	U	A	R	N	U	U	N	N	E
U	O	D	U	I	E	N	R	O	B	N	U
S	N	E	A	V	U	R	T	E	O	U	L
U	K	F	E	U	N	U	N	C	L	O	G
N	N	N	I	N	U	D	U	U	T	U	N
U	U	U	N	T	I	E	D	A	M	N	U

Name/Date _____

Prefixes With Negative Meanings 10

Write the letter of the answer that best matches the meaning of the word.

____ 1. not needed   A. necessary   B. unnecessary

____ 2. not truthful   A. dishonest   B. disbelief

____ 3. unwanted   A. undesirable   B. desirable

____ 4. to stop   A. unavailable   B. discontinue

____ 5. without end   A. limited   B. unlimited

5

Root Word, Prefix, & Suffix Warm-ups: Prefixes With Negative Meanings

Name/Date _____

Prefixes With Negative Meanings 11

Add *in-* or *im-* to each underlined word to form a new word. Use a dictionary if you are not sure which prefix to add.

1. practical _____
2. sincere _____
3. formal _____
4. movable _____
5. appropriate _____
6. capable _____
7. equality _____
8. possible _____
9. flexible _____
10. proper _____

Name/Date _____

Prefixes With Negative Meanings 12

Add *dis-* to each word. On your own paper, write a sentence using each new word.

1. advantage _____
2. approve _____
3. connect _____
4. continue _____
5. prove _____
6. like _____

Name/Date _____

Prefixes With Negative Meanings 13

Answer these questions on your own paper.

1. C*omply* means obey. What does *noncompliance* mean?
2. Give an example of a *non-profit* organization.
3. *Toxic* means poisonous. What does *nontoxic* mean?
4. Give an example of a *nondairy* product.
5. Give an example of a *nonfiction* book.

Name/Date _____

Prefixes With Negative Meanings 14

Complete these on your own paper.

1. Name one thing you are *incapable* of doing.
2. Give an example of *inequality*.
3. Name something that is *inflexible*.
4. Name something that is *impractical*.
5. Name something that is *improper*.
6. Give an example of an *insincere* action.

Name/Date _____

Prefixes With Negative Meanings 15

Write the letter of the answer that best matches the meaning of the word.

____ 1. disadvantage
____ 2. discontinue
____ 3. disconnect
____ 4. disagree
____ 5. disapprove
____ 6. discharge

A. dislike
B. not having the same opinion
C. release
D. stop
E. difficulty
F. take apart

Root Word, Prefix, & Suffix Warm-ups: Prefixes With Negative Meanings

Name/Date _____

Prefixes With Negative Meanings 16

Write the letter of the answer that best matches the definition for each word.

____ 1. impossible   A. likely   B. can't happen

____ 2. impractical   A. wrong   B. not useful

____ 3. improper   A. incorrect B. right

____ 4. inappropriate A. OK   B. unsuitable

____ 5. incapable   A. unable   B. able

____ 6. inequality   A. unhappy B. unfairness

Name/Date _____

Prefixes With Negative Meanings 17

Write the letters from the words in the list on the lines next to the correct definitions.

a. dissatisfied   b. illegible   c. incompetent
d. informal   e. unconscious   f. unfamiliar

____ 1. unaware   ____ 2. strange

____ 3. unhappy   ____ 4. unreadable

____ 5. casual   ____ 6. unskilled

Name/Date _____

Prefixes With Negative Meanings 18

Write 10 words that begin with the prefix non-. Circle the root words.

_____

_____

_____

_____

_____

Name/Date _____

Prefixes With Negative Meanings 19

Write "C" if the word is a compound word. Write "P" if the word includes a prefix. Circle the root words in the words with prefixes.

____ 1. inactive   ____ 2. inaction

____ 3. independent ____ 4. into

____ 5. ingrown   ____ 6. inchworm

____ 7. inside   ____ 8. innkeeper

Name/Date _____

Prefixes With Negative Meanings 20

Circle the word to show what you think. (There are no right or wrong answers.)

1. Getting good grades   Advantage or disadvantage

2. Doing chores at home   Continue or discontinue

3. Going to school on Saturday   Approve or disapprove

4. Learning a second language   Advantage or disadvantage

5. Learning to play the guitar   Advantage or disadvantage

6. Spinach tastes terrific.   Agree or disagree

Root Word, Prefix, & Suffix Warm-ups: Prefixes With Negative Meanings

Name/Date _____

Prefixes With Negative Meanings 21

On another sheet of paper, write a conversation between two people who disagree on something. Use the format shown below. Include at least five statements for each person. Circle all words that include prefixes.

She said, "_____."

He said, "_____."

Name/Date _____

Prefixes With Negative Meanings 22

On another sheet of paper, briefly explain the difference between the words in each pair. Use a dictionary if you need help.

1. nonstop and unstoppable

2. nonhuman and inhuman

3. nonpayment and unpaid

Name/Date _____

Prefixes With Negative Meanings 23

Answer the following questions on your own paper.

1. What does it mean to <u>mistype</u> a word on the computer?

2. If someone wears <u>mismatched</u> socks, what's the problem?

3. If someone <u>misleads</u> you when you ask for directions, what could happen?

4. What can happen if a student <u>misbehaves</u> in school?

5. Why could it be a problem if a secretary <u>misfiles</u> something?

Name/Date _____

Prefixes With Negative Meanings 24

On another sheet of paper, write a short sentence using each word. Use a dictionary if you need help.

1. unavailable
2. unbelievable
3. unusual
4. undesirable
5. unknown
6. unlimited

Name/Date _____

Prefixes With Negative Meanings 25

Draw lines to match the words and their definitions.

1. misshapen   truth
2. mistreat   continuously
3. nonsense   waste
4. nonfiction   twisted
5. nonstop   harm
6. misuse   foolishness

Root Word, Prefix, & Suffix Warm-ups: Prefixes Denoting Numbers

---

Name/Date _____

Prefixes Denoting Numbers 1

Write a poem using the prefixes for the numbers one through ten as the first part of each line. Use "One, Two, Buckle My Shoe" as a model. Be as silly as you like.

uni-, bi-	Unicorns, bipeds, give it a try.
tri-, quad-	_____
penta-, hex-	_____
sept-, oct-	_____
nov-, dec-	_____

Name/Date _____

Prefixes Denoting Numbers 2

Match the words from the list to the definitions.

**centennial   hexagon
octopus   triceratops**

1. a shape with 6 sides   _____
2. a dinosaur with 3 horns _____
3. an animal with 8 arms   _____
4. a 100-year celebration _____

Name/Date _____

Prefixes Denoting Numbers 3

Write the words from the list to match the definitions.

bimonthly   decathlon   quadruplets   quintet

1. 10-sport Olympic event   _____
2. 4 of the same   _____
3. 5 musicians   _____
4. every 2 months   _____

Name/Date _____

Prefixes Denoting Numbers 4

1. How many sides does a <u>decagon</u> have? _____
2. Which is longer, a meter or a <u>millimeter</u>? _____
3. How many <u>millimeters</u> are in a meter? _____
4. Which is longer, a meter or a <u>centimeter</u>? _____
5. How many <u>centimeters</u> are in a meter? _____
6. How many <u>milliliters</u> are in a liter? _____

Name/Date _____

Prefixes Denoting Numbers 5

Circle the correct words to match the definitions. Knowing what the prefixes mean will help.

1.	Knowing two languages	bilateral	bilingual	bicycle
2.	5 Olympic sporting events	pentathlon	quintuplet	pentagon
3.	A 200-year celebration	centennial	biannual	bicentennial
4.	A set of 3 related books or movies	tripod	trilogy	triangle
5.	To cut into 2 pieces	divide	bisect	bicycle
6.	3 of the same	triceratops	triangle	triplets
7.	The 8th month in the Roman calendar	October	August	December

---

Root Word, Prefix, & Suffix Warm-ups: Prefixes Denoting Numbers

Name/Date _____

Prefixes Denoting Numbers 6

1. If you received the first issue of a <u>bimonthly</u> magazine in May, when should the next one arrive? _____

2. If a school held a <u>biannual</u> event in May of 2007, when would the next one be held? _____

3. If a family met for a <u>biennial</u> reunion in July 2007, when did the last reunion occur? _____

4. How often do you think a <u>century</u> plant blooms? _____

5. When will the <u>tricentennial</u> celebration of the United States as a country be held?
_____

Name/Date _____

Prefixes Denoting Numbers 7

Match the letter of the word to its definition.

_____ 1. 3-wheeled vehicle   A. octagon

_____ 2. an animal with 1 horn   B. decade

_____ 3. a stand with 3 legs   C. tripod

_____ 4. a shape with 8 sides   D. biweekly

_____ 5. every 2 weeks   E. unicorn

_____ 6. a period of 10 years   F. tricycle

Name/Date _____

Prefixes Denoting Numbers 8

1. Which has more legs, a <u>centipede</u> or a <u>millipede</u>? _____

2. How many years are in a <u>millennium</u>? _____

3. How many soldiers do you think a Roman <u>centurion</u> commanded? _____

4. Why are some types of eyeglasses called <u>bifocals</u>? _____
_____

Name/Date _____

Prefixes Denoting Numbers 9

On another sheet of paper, write two words using each prefix.

uni-   bi-   tri-   quad-   quin-

penta-   oct-   dec-   cent-   milli-

Name/Date _____

Prefixes Denoting Numbers 10

Write the prefix for each number.

1 _____   2 _____   3 _____

4 _____   5 _____   6 _____

8 _____   10 _____

100 _____   1,000 _____

Root Word, Prefix, & Suffix Warm-ups: Prefixes over- and under-

Name/Date _____

Prefixes over- and under- 1

As a prefix, *under-* can mean: A. beneath; below   B. lower in rank   C. not enough.

For each word, write "A," "B," or "C" to indicate how the prefix *under-* is used.

1. _____ underarm   2. _____ underground   3. _____ underclassman

4. _____ underestimate   5. _____ undersecretary   6. _____ underage

7. _____ underdeveloped   8. _____ underpass   9. _____ underpaid

10. _____ underline   11. _____ undergraduate   12. _____ undercooked

---

Name/Date _____

Prefixes over- and under- 2

Write the answers to these questions on your own paper. Use a dictionary, if necessary.

1. Would you like to go on an undersea adventure? Why or why not?
2. If someone is underhanded, does it mean the person is honest or dishonest?
3. What does it mean if someone is an underdog?
4. If you agree to undertake a big job, what does that mean?

Name/Date _____

Prefixes over- and under- 3

As a prefix, *over-* can have two different meanings.

Write five words that begin with the prefix *over-*, meaning "greatly or completely." *Example:* overjoyed

_____

_____

Write five words that begin with the prefix *over-*, meaning "upper, outer, or above." *Example:* overcoat

_____

_____

Name/Date _____

Prefixes over- and under- 4

Write the answers to these questions on your own paper. Use a dictionary, if necessary.

1. What does it mean to work overtime?
2. What does it mean if someone falls overboard?
3. How do you feel if someone overcharges you at a store?
4. What happens when you overdo exercise?
5. What happens when the bathtub overflows?

Name/Date _____

Prefixes over- and under- 5

1. What's the difference between an overpass and an underpass? _____

_____

2. What's the difference between overpay and underpay? _____

_____

3. Which means an estimate that is too low: overestimate or underestimate? _____

11

Root Word, Prefix, & Suffix Warm-ups: Prefixes

Name/Date _____

Prefixes 1

Answer on your own paper.

1. *Inhale* means to breathe in. What does *exhale* mean?
2. *Include* means to take in. What does *exclude* mean?
3. *Implode* means to burst inward. What does *explode* mean?
4. Give a one-word definition of the prefix *ex-*.

Name/Date _____

Prefixes 2

Answer on your own paper. Use a dictionary if you aren't sure of the answers.

1. What is the difference between *incite* and *excite*?
2. What is the difference between *import* and *export*?
3. What is the difference between *expire* and *inspire*?

Name/Date _____

Prefixes 3

The prefix *hemi-* comes from the Greek word meaning "half." The prefix *semi-* comes from the Latin word meaning "half or partly." Write the answers on your own paper.

1. Draw a semicircle.
2. Do you live in the northern or southern hemisphere?
3. What does it mean to have a semiprivate room in a hospital?

Name/Date _____

Prefixes 4

Micro- and *macro-* are prefixes that mean the opposite. The prefix *macro-* means "huge." The universe is a macrocosm.

Answer on your own paper.

1. What does the prefix *micro-* mean?
2. What is a microcosm?
3. What does a microscope do?

Name/Date _____

_____

Prefixes 5

Add one of these prefixes to each word. Use a dictionary, if you need help finding a word.

micro-   macro-   semi-
hemi-   ex-

Write the new words.

1. private _____
2. change _____
3. professional _____
4. scope _____
5. phone _____
6. circle _____
7. sphere _____
8. colon _____
9. port _____
10. sweet _____
11. final _____
12. conscious _____
13. molecule _____
14. foliate _____
15. cycle _____

12

Root Word, Prefix, & Suffix
Warm-ups: Prefixes

Name/Date _____

Prefixes 6

The prefix *extra-* means "outside or beyond." Write your answers on another sheet of paper. Use a dictionary if you need help.

1. When astronauts go outside of a shuttle in space, it's called an EVA. What does <u>EVA</u> stand for?
2. Some people believe they have ESP. What does <u>ESP</u> stand for?
3. In the movie *E.T.,* what does <u>ET</u> stand for?

Name/Date _____

Prefixes 7

The prefixes *hyper-* and *hypo-* mean the opposite. A person who is hyperactive is extremely active—far above the usual. A person who is hypoactive may move very little. Answer on your own paper.

1. Which prefix means more than normal?
2. Which prefix means less than usual?
3. Would a <u>hypersonic</u> sound be very loud or very soft?
4. When a person suffers from <u>hypothermia</u>, would his temperature be high or low?

Name/Date _____

Prefixes 8

As a prefix, *sub-* can mean:
    A. under, less, or at a lower position
    B. lower in rank C. nearly or approximately

For each word, write "A," "B," or "C" to indicate how the prefix *sub-* is used. Use a dictionary if you need help.

submarine ____ subtropical____ subsoil ____

subway ____ subcommittee ____

subdivide ____ subheading ____ subtotal ____

Name/Date _____

Prefixes 9

1. Which state would be <u>subtropical</u>: Florida or Alaska? _____
2. If you <u>subdivide</u> something, do the pieces get larger or smaller? _____
3. Is a <u>subset</u> smaller or larger than the original set? _____
4. Is the total larger or smaller than the <u>subtotal</u>? _____
5. *Strata* means "a layer." What does *<u>substrata</u>* mean? _____

Name/Date _____

Prefixes 10

Write the prefix on the line next to its meaning.

macro-   extra-   hyper-   micro-   semi-   hypo-   hemi-   ex-   sub-

_____ 1. a prefix meaning from or out   _____ 2. a prefix meaning less than normal

_____ 3. a prefix meaning huge   _____ 4. a prefix meaning lower in rank or below

_____ 5. a prefix meaning tiny   _____ 6. a prefix meaning more than normal

_____ 7. Latin prefix for half   _____ 8. a prefix meaning outside or beyond

_____ 9. Greek prefix meaning half

Root Word, Prefix, & Suffix Warm-ups: Prefixes

Name/Date _____

Prefixes 11

The prefix *inter-* means "between or among." The prefix *intra-* means "inside or within." Circle the correct word for each item.

1. To exchange gifts between two people   interchange or intrachange

2. Sporting events between teams from different schools   intermural or intramural

3. Sporting events between teams in the same school   intermural or intramural

4. A highway that covers more than one state   interstate or intrastate

5. Shipping from one city to another inside the same state   interstate or intrastate

6. A flight from New York to London   intercontinental or intracontinental

---

Name/Date _____

Prefixes 12

Write the answers on your own paper.

1. Write a short definition for <u>interaction</u>.
2. *Com* means to speak. What is an <u>intercom</u>?
3. What do the letters <u>IV</u> stand for (medical definition)?
4. Write a short definition for the <u>Internet</u>.
5. Draw three <u>interlocking</u> circles.

Name/Date _____

Prefixes 13

The prefixes *pre-* and *post-* have opposite meanings. Write the answers on your own paper.

1. Which comes first, the <u>pregame</u> show or the <u>postgame</u> show?
2. What is a <u>preview</u> of a movie?
3. When someone writes <u>PS</u> at the end of a letter, what does it stand for and what does it mean?
4. What does the prefix *pre-* mean?
5. What does the prefix *post-* mean?

Name/Date _____

Prefixes 14

Answer on your own paper.
1. About how old would someone be who attends <u>preschool</u>?
2. Would it be likely that someone under 16 takes <u>postgraduate</u> courses? Why or why not?
3. Name a <u>prehistoric</u> animal.
4. What does <u>prehistoric</u> mean?
5. Would a woman go to a doctor for <u>postnatal</u> care before or after the baby was born?

Name/Date _____

Prefixes 15

Divide a sheet of paper into four columns. Write words that begin with a different prefix in each column. Select any prefixes to use. Try to list at least ten words for each prefix.

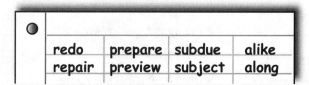

| redo | prepare | subdue | alike |
| repair | preview | subject | along |

14

Root Word, Prefix, & Suffix
Warm-ups: Prefixes

Name/Date _____

Prefixes 16

The prefix *mega-* can mean either "1,000 of something" or "very large."

1. There are about 1,000 species of bats. They are divided into two groups: <u>megabats</u> and <u>microbats</u>. Which group represents the larger bats? _____

2. How many bytes are in a <u>megabyte</u>? _____

3. Write another word that begins with the prefix *mega-*. _____

Name/Date _____

Prefixes 17

The prefix *de-* can mean "down or away." It can also mean "to remove or reverse." On your own paper, write a short definition for each word. Use a dictionary if you need help.

1. descend   2. debug
3. delay   4. deduce
5. decline   6. demerit
7. deduct

Name/Date _____

Prefixes 18

On your own paper, briefly describe the difference between each pair of words. Use a dictionary if you need help.

1. decline and incline

2. increase and decrease

3. inflate and deflate

4. deactivate and reactivate

Name/Date _____

Prefixes 19

Answer on your own paper.

1. Edward Gibbon wrote *The History of the Decline and Fall of the Roman Empire*. What is the difference between <u>decline</u> and <u>fall</u>?

2. If you want to take moisture (humidity) from the air, would you use a <u>humidifier</u> or a <u>dehumidifier</u>?

3. If a king is <u>dethroned</u>, would he continue as ruler of the country?

Name/Date _____

Prefixes 20

Circle "T" for true or "F" for false.

1. T F To exhale means to take a deep breath and hold it.
2. T F All prehistoric animals were dinosaurs.
3. T F Scientists can learn much by studying prehistoric writing.
4. T F If a person has hypersensitive hearing, she can hear very well.
5. T F A child who is hyperactive can rarely sit still.
6. T F Postoperative care means care after an operation.
7. T F When you buy something, the subtotal is the amount before taxes are added.

Root Word, Prefix, & Suffix
Warm-ups: Prefixes

Name/Date _____

Prefixes 21

1. If an item is <u>preassembled</u> when you buy it, do you have to put it together yourself? _____

2. If the Egyptian Empire <u>predates</u> the Roman Empire, which came first? _____

3. If something is <u>submerged</u>, is it above or below the water? _____

4. <u>Micronesia</u> is a group of islands in the Pacific Ocean. Are they large or small? _____

Name/Date _____

Prefixes 22

Write two words that begin with each prefix.

1. *sub-* _____

2. *pre-* _____

3. *micro-* _____

4. *semi-* _____

5. *hyper-* _____

Name/Date _____

Prefixes 23

Match the definitions to the prefixes from this list.

pre-   over-   macro-   sub-   micro-   hyper-   re-   mis-

1. before _____   2. huge _____   3. not _____

4. tiny _____   5. again _____   6. above _____

7. more than normal _____   8. lower in rank or below _____

Name/Date _____

Prefixes 24

Match the definitions to the prefixes.

_____ 1. from or out

_____ 2. very large

_____ 3. less than normal

_____ 4. outside or beyond

_____ 5. not enough

_____ 6. after

_____ 7. not

A. un-
B. extra-
C. mega-
D. post-
E. hypo-
F. under-
G. ex-

Name/Date _____

Prefixes 25

Write one of these prefixes on the blank before each word to make a new word. Some root words may work with more than one prefix.

*de-   ex-   extra-   hyper-   hypo-   inter-
intra-   macro-   mega-   micro-   post-   pre-*

1. _____activate   2. _____state

3. _____formed   4. _____register

5. _____part   6. _____phone

7. _____port   8. _____active

Root Word, Prefix, & Suffix
Warm-ups: Prefix Review

Name/Date _____

Prefix Review 1

Circle the prefix in each word. Underline the root words.

1. disagree	2. distrust	3. insincere	4. incorrect	5. indirect
6. immortal	7. impolite	8. misfit	9. mistrust	10. nonstop
11. nonprofit	12. overhead	13. overheat	14. overweight	15. unhappy
16. unselfish	17. underfoot	18. underline	19. replace	20. illegal

---

Name/Date _____

Prefix Review 2

On another sheet of paper, write ten words using a prefix that has a number meaning, such as *tri-* or *quad-*. Write a short definition for each word.

Name/Date _____

Prefix Review 3

Write the letter of the answer that matches.

____ 1. Prefix that means *eight*   A. quad-

____ 2. Prefix that means *five*   B. bi-

____ 3. Prefix that means *four*   C. uni-

____ 4. Prefix that means *one*   D. oct-

____ 5. Prefix that means *three*   E. penta-

____ 6. Prefix that means *two*   F. tri-

Name/Date _____

Prefix Review 4

Add *un-, dis-, in-, il-,* or *im-* to each adjective. On another sheet of paper, write a short sentence for each new word that shows you understand the meaning of the word. Use a dictionary if needed.

1. ____familiar   2. ____formal

3. ____legible   4. ____practical

5. ____satisfied   6. ____tolerable

Name/Date _____

Prefix Review 5

On another sheet of paper, explain the difference between each pair of words.

1. unable and disable
2. mislay and relay
3. nonstop and unstoppable
4. reset and unset
5. uncap and recap
6. repaid and unpaid

Root Word, Prefix, & Suffix
Warm-ups: Prefix Review

Name/Date _____

Prefix Review 6

Does the word contain a prefix? Write "yes" or "no" on the line.

_____ 1. uncle   _____ 2. illness

_____ 3. uncap   _____ 4. illogical

_____ 5. unclear   _____ 6. dishes

_____ 7. unite   _____ 8. distrust

_____ 9. untie   _____ 10. misses

_____ 11. ready   _____ 12. none

Name/Date _____

Prefix Review 7

On another sheet of paper, explain the difference between each pair of words.

1. miscalculate and recalculate
2. disorder and reorder
3. bicentennial and biannual
4. removed and unmoved
5. pentathlon and decathlon
6. quintuplets and quadruplets

Name/Date _____

Prefix Review 8

Match the words and definitions.

____ 1. bilingual   ____ 2. bisect   ____ 3. biweekly

____ 4. inflexible   ____ 5. informal   ____ 6. nonfiction

____ 7. octogenarian   ____ 8. trilogy   ____ 9. triplets   ____ 10. tripod

A. relaxed; casual   B. three of the same   C. a person who is 80 years old
D. every two weeks   E. to cut into two pieces   F. a three-legged stand
G. three related books or movies   H. truth   I. hard; firm
J. knowing two languages

Name/Date _____

Prefix Review 9

Add a prefix to each root word.

1. _____loyal   2. _____annual

3. _____color   4. _____cycle

5. _____sphere   6. _____done

7. _____use   8. _____think

9. _____paint   10. _____place

Name/Date _____

Prefix Review 10

Match the words and definitions.

_____ 1. dissatisfied   A. harm
_____ 2. impossible   B. below the water
_____ 3. impractical   C. new and strange
_____ 4. insincere   D. unhappy
_____ 5. misshapen   E. twisted
_____ 6. mistreat   F. can't happen
_____ 7. undersea   G. not truthful
_____ 8. unfamiliar   H. not useful

18

Root Word, Prefix, & Suffix Warm-ups: Prefix Review

Name/Date _____

Prefix Review 11

Write the meaning of each prefix.

1. extra- _____   2. macro- _____
3. sub- _____   4. inter- _____
5. intra- _____   6. pre- _____
7. post- _____   8. mega- _____
9. micro- _____   10. de- _____

Name/Date _____

Prefix Review 12

Write two words that begin with each prefix.

1. de- _____
2. extra- _____
3. inter- _____
4. intra- _____
5. micro- _____
6. post- _____
7. pre- _____
8. sub- _____

Name/Date _____

Prefix Review 13

Circle the root words.

1. derail   2. debug   3. intramural
4. interstate 5. subdivide 6. preexisting
7. demerit   8. postgame   9. subway
10. microscope   11. megaphone
12. extraordinary   13. megacycle
14. deport   15. submarine

Name/Date _____

Prefix Review 14

Cut or photocopy an article from a newspaper or download one from the Internet. Circle all words in the article that contain a prefix. On your own paper, make a list of the words you circled.

Name/Date _____

Prefix Review 15

1. Which are larger: microorganisms or megaorganisms? _____
2. If you export goods, does it mean you buy from or sell to another country? _____
3. Would a flight from Canada to Mexico be intercontinental or intracontinental?

_____
4. Would megasaurus be a good name for a small dinosaur? _____
5. Does prehistory mean before or after written history? _____
6. An example of an interplanetary trip would be from _____ to _____.

Root Word, Prefix, & Suffix
Warm-ups: Prefix Review

Name/Date _____

Prefix Review 16

Circle "T" for true or "F" for false.

1. T   F   The meaning of a word changes when a prefix is added.
2. T   F   Prefixes only appear at the beginning of words.
3. T   F   Adding a prefix usually changes the part of speech of a word.
4. T   F   A word cannot include both a prefix and a suffix.
5. T   F   A prefix is added to the end of a word.
6. T   F   A word can have two or more prefixes.
7. T   F   The spelling of a root word usually doesn't change when a prefix is added.

Name/Date _____

Prefix Review 17

Add a prefix to each word.

1. _____move   2. _____like
3. _____usual   4. _____appoint
5. _____sense   6. _____cycle
7. _____loyal   8. _____equal
9. _____color   10. _____charge

Name/Date _____

Prefix Review 18

Write 12 words that include prefixes, changing a word to its antonym.
Examples: happy – unhappy; stop – nonstop

_____
_____
_____
_____

Name/Date _____

Prefix Review 19

Write 12 words that include a prefix, denoting a number. *Examples:* biplane, tricolor

_____
_____
_____
_____

Name/Date _____

Prefix Review 20

Complete the following on your own paper.

1. Draw a semicircle.   2. Draw a submarine.
3. Draw a globe. Show where the southern hemisphere is located.
4. Draw four interlocking circles.
5. Draw a pentagon.   6. Draw a tripod.
7. List three months that include a prefix.
8. Write a PS to a letter.

Root Word, Prefix, & Suffix Warm-ups: Adding Suffixes

Name/Date _____

Adding Suffixes 1

Adding a suffix to a root word changes the meaning of the word. Sometimes the spelling of the root word also changes. Write two more examples for each rule below.

- For words ending in *e*, drop the *e* and add the suffix if the suffix begins with a vowel.
  Examples: expire + ation = expiration   wise + est = wisest   observe + ance = observance

1. _____

- For short words with the consonant/vowel/consonant (CVC) pattern, double the final consonant before adding the suffix. *Examples:* hot + est = hottest   sad + er = sadder

2. _____

Name/Date _____

Adding Suffixes 2

Write two more examples of each rule.

- For most words ending in *y* preceded by a vowel, simply add the suffix.
  Examples: joy + ous = joyous   buy + er = buyer

1. _____

- For most words ending in *y* preceded by a consonant, change the *y* to *i* and add the suffix.
  Examples: try + ed = tried   icy + est = iciest

2. _____

Name/Date _____

Adding Suffixes 3

Answer on your own paper.

1. Even if you know the spelling guidelines, why is it a good idea to check a dictionary if you are unsure of the correct spelling of a word?

2. Why is it a good idea to check a dictionary if you are unsure of the meaning of a word?

Name/Date _____

Adding Suffixes 4

Circle the root words if the spelling will change when a suffix beginning with a vowel is added.

beauty	big	bumpy	busy
carry	desire	direct	tall
fluffy	wet	greasy	magnify
rapid	short	slow	ugly

Name/Date _____

Adding Suffixes 5

On your own paper, write the root word for each word below. Use a dictionary if you aren't sure of the spelling.

1. adoption
2. agreement
3. stylish
4. combination
5. daily
6. decoration
7. directions
8. government
9. invitation
10. twitching

Root Word, Prefix, & Suffix
Warm-ups: Suffixes -er, -or, -est

Name/Date _____

Suffixes -er, -or, -est 1

When the suffix *-er* is added to an adjective, it means "more." *Example:* quick + er = quicker. Review spelling rules. Add *-er* to each word, and write new words.

1. hot _____
2. sad _____
3. cold _____
4. tasty _____
5. funny _____
6. red _____
7. high _____
8. dry _____

Name/Date _____

Suffixes -er, -or, -est 2

Write ten other adjectives not used in Activity 1 that end in *-er*.

_____

_____

_____

_____

_____

Name/Date _____

Suffixes -er, -or, -est 3

When the suffix *-est* is added to an adjective, it means "most." *Example:* quick + est = quickest. Review spelling rules. Add *-est* and write the new words.

1. speedy _____
2. wise _____
3. close _____
4. jolly _____
5. tiny _____
6. wet _____
7. fresh _____
8. old _____
9. spicy _____

10. When *-er* is added to an adjective, is the new word an adjective? _____

11. When *-est* is added to an adjective, is the new word an adjective? _____

Name/Date _____

Suffixes -er, -or, -est 4

Adding the suffix *-er* or *-or* to a verb changes it to a noun. *Examples:* act + or = actor; play + er = player Add *-er* or *-or* to each verb, and write the new words. Check a dictionary if you are not sure which suffix to use.

1. bake _____
2. direct _____
3. golf _____
4. govern _____
5. jog _____
6. sing _____
7. manage _____
8. write _____

Name/Date _____

Suffixes -er, -or, –est 5

1. What do the suffixes *-er* and *-or* mean?

_____

2. Write ten other verbs not used in Activity 4 that change to nouns by adding *-er* or *-or*.

_____

_____

_____

_____

Root Word, Prefix, & Suffix
Warm-ups: Suffixes -ly and -ful

Name/Date _____

Suffixes -ly and -ful 1

On your own paper, add *-ly* to change the adjectives to adverbs. Review spelling guidelines for words that end in *y*.

1. neat	2. slow	3. fierce	4. happy
5. grateful	6. glad	7. loud	8. nervous
9. smart	10. rare	11. short	12. noisy

Name/Date _____

Suffixes -ly and -ful 2

Adding the suffix *-ly* to an adjective changes it to an adverb. On another sheet of paper, write a short sentence using the adverb form of each of the words listed.

Please

THANK YOU

1. broad	2. polite	3. quick
4. quiet	5. rude	6. sad
7. shy	8. silent	9. timid
		10. weak

Name/Date _____

Suffixes -ly and -ful 3

The words *thoughtful, trustful,* and *handful* include the suffix *-ful*. Answer the following on your own paper.

1. What does the suffix *-ful* mean?
2. Write six more words that end with the suffix *-ful*.
3. Write a sentence using two words that end in *-ful*.

Name/Date _____

Suffixes -ly and -ful 4

Add the suffix *-ful* to each of these words, and write the new words on the lines below.

1. color _____
2. faith _____
3. grace _____
4. hope _____
5. plenty _____
6. play _____

Name/Date _____

_____

Suffixes -ly and -ful 5

Match the words ending in *-ful* with their definitions. Use a dictionary if you need help.

_____ 1. boastful

_____ 2. cheerful

_____ 3. doubtful

_____ 4. dreadful

_____ 5. dutiful

_____ 6. fanciful

_____ 7. flavorful

_____ 8. tearful

_____ 9. truthful

_____ 10. harmful

A. honest

B. imaginative

C. sad

D. risky

E. tasty

F. proud

G. terrible

H. happy

I. unsure

J. obedient

Root Word, Prefix, & Suffix
Warm-ups: Suffixes -less, -tion, -ation

Name/Date _____

Suffixes -less, -tion, -ation 1

The words *helpless, fearless,* and *friendless* include the suffix *-less.*

1. What does the suffix *-less* mean?

   _____

2. On your own paper, write six other words that end in *-less.* Include a short definition for each word.

Name/Date _____

Suffixes -less, -tion, -ation 2

Answer on your own paper.

1. Do you prefer foods that are <u>tasteless</u> or <u>tasteful</u>?
2. Is a good dancer <u>graceless</u> or <u>graceful</u>?
3. Are you a <u>careless</u> person or a <u>careful</u> one?
4. Does <u>endless</u> mean eternal or brief?
5. If something is <u>flawless</u>, does it have few errors or no errors?
6. Why were early cars called "<u>horseless</u> carriages"?

Name/Date _____

Suffixes -less, -tion, -ation 3

The suffixes *-tion* and *-ation* change words from verbs to nouns.
Example: adore + ation = adoration
On another sheet of paper, add *-tion* or *-ation* to each verb. Write a short definition for the word and use it in a sentence. Use a dictionary if you are unsure of the spelling or definition.

1. donate   2. admire
3. regulate   4. cooperate   5. inspire

Name/Date _____

Suffixes -less, -tion, -ation 4

On your own paper, write the root words.

1. action   2. adoption
3. exception   4. direction
5. beautification   6. creation
7. capitalization   8. subtraction
9. reduction   10. clarification
11. contraction   12. imagination

Name/Date _____

Suffixes -less, -tion, -ation 5

Match the words to their definitions. Use a dictionary if you need help.

A. the process of learning   B. to ask   C. a group of things   D. ornaments
E. to make something look nice   F. to teach   G. a request to attend or meet
H. to join two or more things   I. to acquire   J. the bringing of a child into one's family

____ 1. adopt ____ 2. invite ____ 3. adoption ____ 4. combine ____ 5. combination

____ 6. educate ____ 7. decorate ____ 8. decorations ____ 9. education ____ 10. invitation

Root Word, Prefix, & Suffix Warm-ups: Suffixes -able and -ment

Name/Date _____

Suffixes -able and -ment 1

Acceptable, workable, and *taxable* end with the suffix *-able.* Add the suffix *-able* to each word below, and write the new words. Keep spelling guidelines in mind.

1. avoid _____
2. bear _____
3. beat _____
4. bend _____
5. compare _____
6. correct _____
7. inflate _____
8. like _____
9. love _____
10. remove _____
11. respect _____
12. use _____
13. What does the suffix *-able* mean? _____

Name/Date _____

Suffixes -able and -ment 2

Answer on your own paper.

1. Name something that is <u>chewable</u>.
2. Give an example of something people wear that is <u>fashionable</u>.
3. Name an organization that is <u>charitable</u>.
4. What kind of weather is <u>favorable</u> for a parade?
5. What does "<u>payable</u> on demand" mean?
6. What would you like to have that is not <u>affordable</u> to you right now?

Name/Date _____

Suffixes -able and -ment 3

Add the suffix *-able* to each word and use it in a sentence. Write your answers on another sheet of paper. Use a dictionary if you are unsure of the meaning or spelling of a word.

adapt	comfort
compare	debate
remove	desire
favor	charge pass respect

Name/Date _____

Suffixes -able and -ment 4

Adding the suffix *-ment* changes words from verbs to nouns. Add *-ment* to each word. Write the new word and a short definition for each word on your own paper.

DON'T MISS OUT!
INVESTMENT
OPPORTUNITY!
INFO MEETING 7 PM TONIGHT!

adjust	advertise	
amuse	assign	excite
judge	manage	pay

Name/Date _____

Suffixes -able and -ment 5

Answer on your own paper.

1. Give an example of something that would cause <u>excitement</u> in your school.
2. Name one type of <u>treatment</u> for a cold.
3. Name something about which you and your parents are in <u>agreement</u>.
4. Name something that causes you <u>amazement</u>.
5. What is something you feel is a great <u>accomplishment</u>?

Root Word, Prefix, & Suffix Warm-ups: Suffixes -ology, -ist, -phobia

Name/Date _____

Suffixes -ology, -ist, -phobia 1

The suffix *-ology* means the "study of." Use a dictionary or the Internet to find out about these *-ologies*.
Example: Criminology is the study of crimes and criminals.

1. Biology is the study of _____.

2. Zoology is the study of _____.

3. Mythology is the study of _____.

4. Geology is the study of _____.

5. Anthropology is the study of _____.

6. Psychology is the study of _____.

7. Archaeology is the study of _____.

8. Ichthyology is the study of _____.

Name/Date _____

Suffixes -ology, -ist, -phobia 2

The suffix *-ist* is often used to mean "someone who knows how to do something."
Example: A flutist knows how to play a flute.

1. A botanist is one who knows about _____.

2. A florist knows about _____.

3. A dentist takes care of _____.

4. A harpist knows how to play the _____.

5. A person who has studied biology would be a _____.

Name/Date _____

Suffixes -ology, -ist, -phobia 3

1. What subject does a chemist know about?
_____

2. What does a cyclist ride? _____

3. What is the word for someone who plays the piano? _____

4. What does a therapist do? _____

5. What does a typist do well? _____

6. What does a meteorologist study? _____
_____

Name/Date _____

Suffixes -ology, -ist, -phobia 4

The suffix *-phobia* means "fear of" something. Use a dictionary or the Internet to find out about these phobias.

1. Acrophobia means fear of _____.

2. Apiphobia means fear of _____.

3. Hydrophobia means fear of _____.

4. Heliophobia means fear of _____.

5. Phobophobia means fear of _____.

Name/Date _____

Suffixes -ology, -ist, -phobia 5

On another sheet of paper, make up ten phobias and explain what they mean.

Example: Myrtlephobia
– fear of women named Myrtle.

Root Word, Prefix, & Suffix
Warm-ups: Suffixes -ish, -ness, -an

Name/Date _____

Suffixes -ish, -ness, -an 1

On your own paper, add the suffix -ish to each word. Write a short definition for the new words.

1. baby   2. blue   3. child

4. green   5. red   6. style

Name/Date _____

Suffixes -ish, -ness, -an 2

Add the suffix -ness to each word and write the new word. Review spelling guidelines for words ending in y.

1. dizzy _____   2. easy _____

3. firm _____   4. lazy _____

5. lonely _____   6. meek _____

Name/Date _____

Suffixes -ish, -ness, -an 3

Write words from the list to match the definitions.

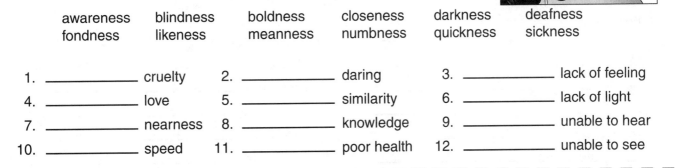

awareness   blindness   boldness   closeness   darkness   deafness
fondness   likeness   meanness   numbness   quickness   sickness

1. _____ cruelty   2. _____ daring   3. _____ lack of feeling

4. _____ love   5. _____ similarity   6. _____ lack of light

7. _____ nearness   8. _____ knowledge   9. _____ unable to hear

10. _____ speed   11. _____ poor health 12. _____ unable to see

---

Name/Date _____

Suffixes -ish, -ness, -an 4

The suffixes -ish and -an, combined with part of a country name, are commonly used to denote nationality or language. Example: A person from Great Britain is British. Use a dictionary if you need help.

1. A person from Sweden is _____.
2. A person from Australia is _____.
3. In Turkey, people speak _____.
4. People from Finland speak _____.
5. People from Rome were called _____.

Name/Date _____

Suffixes -ish, -ness, -an 5

1. The language of Spain is _____.
2. People from Egypt are _____.
3. In Italy, people speak _____.
4. People from Hawaii are _____.
5. People in Russia speak _____.
6. People from Poland speak _____.
7. A person from Mexico is _____.
8. People from Ireland are _____.

Root Word, Prefix, & Suffix Warm-ups: Words With Prefixes & Suffixes

Name/Date _____

Words With Prefixes & Suffixes 1

Underline the prefixes and suffixes in each word. Write the root words on the lines.

1. direction _____
2. directive _____
3. director _____
4. directory _____
5. investigate _____
6. investigation _____
7. investigator _____
8. investor _____
9. observance _____
10. observation _____
11. observatory _____
12. observer _____
13. proposal _____
14. proposition _____
15. reinvest _____

Name/Date _____

Words With Prefixes & Suffixes 2

Add a prefix and one or more suffixes to each word. Write the new words.
Example: un + luck + y = unlucky

1. like _____
2. happy _____
3. invest _____
4. detect _____
5. cooperate _____

Name/Date _____

Words With Prefixes & Suffixes 3

Use a dictionary to write short definitions for words based on the word *alter*.

alter – (v.) to change

1. alteration _____
2. alternate _____
3. alternately _____
4. alternative _____
5. unaltered _____

Name/Date _____

Words With Prefixes & Suffixes 4

On another sheet of paper, write a short sentence for each word based on the words *consider* and *cooperate*. Use a dictionary if you are not sure of the meaning.

consider – (v.) to think about; to ponder
cooperate – (v.) to get along; to work together

1. considerable
2. consideration
3. inconsiderate
4. reconsider
5. cooperation
6. cooperative
7. uncooperative

Name/Date _____

Words With Prefixes & Suffixes 5

On the tree branches, write five or more words made by adding prefixes and/or suffixes to the root word.

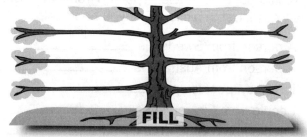

FILL

28

Root Word, Prefix, & Suffix Warm-ups: Words With Prefixes & Suffixes

---

Name/Date _____

Words With Prefixes & Suffixes 6

Answer on your own paper.

1. If you could make an <u>alteration</u> to the place where you live, what would you change?
2. What are two <u>alternative</u> options for something fun to do on a Saturday?
3. How do you feel about people who are <u>inconsiderate</u> of others?
4. What do you spend <u>considerable</u> energy doing?
5. Name a person who is very <u>cooperative</u>.

Name/Date _____

Words With Prefixes & Suffixes 7

Use a dictionary to write short definitions for words based on the word *direct*.

direct – (v) to lead

1. directive _____
2. directly _____
3. director _____
4. misdirection _____
5. indirect _____

Name/Date _____

Words With Prefixes & Suffixes 8

Write the letter of the correct word for each definition given.

_____ 1. a great amount   A. reconsider   B. considerable   C. consideration
_____ 2. a joint effort   A. cooperate   B. cooperation   C. cooperative
_____ 3. on the other hand   A. alteration   B. alternate   C. alternately
_____ 4. selfish   A. inconsiderate   B. reconsider   C. considerable
_____ 5. unchanged   A. altered   B. unaltered   C. alternate
_____ 6. unhelpful   A. cooperation   B. cooperative   C. uncooperative
_____ 7. unnoticeable   A. undetectable   B. detection   C. detective

---

Name/Date _____

Words With Prefixes and Suffixes 9

Adding prefixes and suffixes changes the part of speech of a word. Write "N" if the word is a noun, "V" if it is a verb, or "A" if it is an adjective.

1. alteration _____   2. direction _____
3. inconsiderate _____   4. unaltered _____
5. considerable _____   6. consider _____
7. director _____   8. cooperate _____
9. cooperation _____   10. reconsider _____

Name/Date _____

Words With Prefixes and Suffixes 10

On the tree branches, write five or more words made by adding prefixes and/or suffixes to the root word.

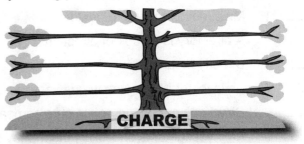

CHARGE

29

Root Word, Prefix, & Suffix Warm-ups: Words With Prefixes & Suffixes

---

Name/Date _____

Words With Prefixes and Suffixes 11

On another sheet of paper, write a short sentence using each word listed below that is based on the word *invest*. Use a dictionary if you are not sure of the meaning.

invest – put time, money, energy, etc., into something in the hope that it will pay off later

investigate   investigation   investigator

investor   reinvest   investment

Name/Date _____

Words With Prefixes and Suffixes 12

On another sheet of paper, list as many words as you can that end in *-tion* or *-ation*. Then, write a short silly poem about an investigation into a transgression (crime) in a cookie factory.

Name/Date _____

Words With Prefixes and Suffixes 13

Adding prefixes and suffixes changes the part of speech of a word. Write "N" if the word is a noun, "V" if it is a verb, or "A" if it is an adjective.

____ 1. direct   ____ 2. directory

____ 3. invest   ____ 4. investigate

____ 5. investigation   ____ 6. investigator

____ 7. investor   ____ 8. reinvest

____ 9. removable   ____ 10. remove

Name/Date _____

Words With Prefixes and Suffixes 14

On the tree branches, write five or more words made by adding prefixes and/or suffixes to the root word.

FRIEND

Name/Date _____

Words With Prefixes and Suffixes 15

Write "T" for true or "F" for false.

____ 1. Misdirection means to get lost.   ____ 2. A directive is an order or command.

____ 3. A directory is a book of directions.   ____ 4. A director is one who leads.

____ 5. Directly means soon.   ____ 6. An investigation is a study of something.

____ 7. An investor is one who wears vests.   ____ 8. To investigate means to look into something.

____ 9. Directions can mean points on a compass or instructions.

____ 10. An investigator is one who puts money into a project.

Root Word, Prefix, & Suffix Warm-ups: Words With Prefixes & Suffixes

Name/Date _____

Words With Prefixes and Suffixes 16

Match these words listed below to their meanings. The words are all based on the word *observe.* Use a dictionary if you are not sure of the definitions.

_____ 1. observance

_____ 2. observant

_____ 3. observation

_____ 4. observatory

_____ 5. observer

_____ 6. nonobservance

A. close study

B. the act of following laws or customs

C. failure to follow a custom, such as celebrating a holiday

D. one who watches

E. alert, attentive

F. a place to watch the stars and planets

Name/Date _____

Words With Prefixes and Suffixes 17

On your own paper, write a short definition of each word derived from the word *detect.* Use a dictionary if needed.

detect – (v) to find
1. detection
2. detective
3. detector
4. undetectable

Name/Date _____

Words With Prefixes and Suffixes 18

Adding prefixes and suffixes changes the part of speech of a word. Write "N" if the word is a noun, "V" if it is a verb, or "A" if it is an adjective.

_____ 1. detect

_____ 3. detector

_____ 5. observation

_____ 7. observe

_____ 9. undetectable

_____ 2. detection

_____ 4. observance

_____ 6. observatory

_____ 8. observer

_____ 10. unobserved

Name/Date _____

Words With Prefixes and Suffixes 19

On the tree branches, write five or more words made by adding prefixes and/or suffixes to the root word.

LOVE

Name/Date _____

Words With Prefixes and Suffixes 20

Cut or copy an article from a newspaper or download one from the Internet. Circle all words in the article that contain a prefix and/or suffix. On your own paper, make a list of the words you circled.

SEARCH:
COMPUTER
NEWSPAPER
ENCYCLOPEDIA
DICTIONARY
MAGAZINE
SOURCES

Root Word, Prefix, & Suffix
Warm-ups: Suffix Review

Name/Date _____

Suffix Review 1

Does the spelling of the root word change when the suffix is added? Circle "yes" or "no." If yes, write the new word.

1. beauty + -ful   yes   no   _____
2. desire + -able   yes   no   _____
3. equip + -ment   yes   no   _____
4. except + -ion   yes   no   _____
5. happy + -ly   yes   no   _____
6. icy + -est   yes   no   _____

Name/Date _____

Suffix Review 2

Add a suffix to each word. Write the new word and a short definition on another sheet of paper.

therapy	geology
inflate	adapt
judge	manage

Name/Date _____

Suffix Review 3

Circle the 21 -er and -or words hidden in the puzzle.

```
V D I N E R E K A B
E O A R A R E C A R
N E T N E R T A A B
D R G E C O B M E W
O E O R R E V A E W
R L R O R R R Y D E
E D R O V E R O I L
V D N F R X E R T D
I O R E M R A F O E
D T A R E T N E R R
```

ACTOR	DONOR	ROOFER
BAKER	EDITOR	ROVER
BARBER	FARMER	TODDLER
BEARER	MAYOR	VENDOR
DANCER	RACER	VOTER
DINER	RANGER	WEAVER
DIVER	RENTER	WELDER

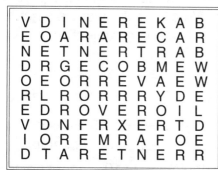

Name/Date _____

Suffix Review 4

On another sheet of paper, write three or more couplets (two-line rhyming poems) using any words that end in -er or -or.

Examples: The miner felt finer
After he ate at the diner.

I said to the baker,
"Please pass the salt shaker."

Name/Date _____

Suffix Review 5

Circle "T" for true or "F" for false.

T   F   1. A proposition is a suggestion or plan.
T   F   2. To observe can mean to watch the stars.
T   F   3. To be observant means to pay attention to details.
T   F   4. A proposal is a promise.
T   F   5. An observer is one who is lost.
T   F   6. To propose means to ask someone to marry you.

Root Word, Prefix, & Suffix
Warm-ups: Suffix Review

Name/Date _____

Suffix Review 6

Write the answers from the list of suffixes:

-able   -er   -ful   -ish   -less   -ly   -ology   -phobia

_____ 1. Suffix that changes adjectives to adverbs

_____ 3. Suffix that means "somewhat like"

_____ 5. Suffix that means "filled with"

_____ 7. Suffix that means "one who"

_____ 2. Suffix that means "able to"

_____ 4. Suffix that means "fear of"

_____ 6. Suffix that means "lack of"

_____ 8. Suffix that means "study of"

Name/Date _____

Suffix Review 7

Answer on your own paper.
1. When -er or -or is added to a verb, is the new word a verb or a noun?
2. Write two examples of question 1.
3. When -er is added to an adjective, is the new word an adjective or an adverb?
4. Write two examples of question 3.
5. When -est is added to an adjective, is the new word a noun or an adjective?
6. Write two examples of question 5.

Name/Date _____

Suffix Review 8

Does the spelling of the root word change when the suffix is added? Circle "yes" or "no." If yes, write the new word.

1. joy + -ous   yes no _____
2. move + -able   yes no _____
3. penny + -less   yes no _____
4. sense + -less   yes no _____
5. sense + -or   yes no _____
6. style + -ish   yes no _____

Name/Date _____

Suffix Review 9

Answer on your own paper.
1. When -ly is added to an adjective, is the new word an adverb or an adjective?
2. Write two examples of question 1.
3. When -tion or -ation is added to a verb, is the new word an adjective or a noun?
4. Write two examples of question 3.
5. When -ment is added to a verb, is the new word a verb or a noun?
6. Write two examples of question 5.

Name/Date _____

Suffix Review 10

On the tree branches, write five or more words made by adding prefixes and/or suffixes to the root word.

PAY

Root Word, Prefix, & Suffix
Warm-ups: Final Review

Name/Date _____

Final Review 1

Answer on your own paper.

1. Write three examples of prefixes.
2. Write three examples of suffixes.
3. Write three words that include prefixes.
4. Write three words that include suffixes.
5. Write three words that include prefixes and suffixes.

Name/Date _____

Final Review 2

Work with a partner. Make a list of words that end in *-tion* or *-ation*. Use the words to write three phrases and their definitions. Write the answers on your own paper.

Examples:

Dalmatian plantation = Home of "101 Dalmatians"

Generation altercation = A disagreement between a grandparent and grandchild

Carnation congregation = A flower show

Name/Date _____

Final Review 3

Write the letter of the correct answer on the line.

_____	1.	a great amount	A. reconsider	B. considerable	C. consideration
_____	2.	a joint effort	A. cooperate	B. cooperation	C. cooperatively
_____	3.	cannot be obtained	A. unbelievable	B. available	C. unavailable
_____	4.	lack of faith or trust	A. belief	B. disbelief	C. unavailable
_____	5.	not needed	A. necessary	B. dishonest	C. unnecessary
_____	6.	not truthful	A. dishonest	B. honest	C. disbelief
_____	7.	on the other hand	A. alteration	B. alternate	C. alternately

---

Name/Date _____

Final Review 4

Write the words from the list to match the definitions.

boldness   disorder   disrepair
disrespectful   fairness   quickness

_____ justice   _____ daring

_____ speed   _____ rude

_____ chaos

_____ falling
              apart

Name/Date _____

Final Review 5

Match the words with their definitions.

____	1. bilingual	A. sad
____	2. disconnect	B. truth
____	3. mislay	C. a shape with 4 sides
____	4. nonfiction	D. take apart
____	5. observant	E. knowing two
____	6. pentagon	languages
____	7. quadrilateral	F. alert, attentive
____	8. tearful	G. a shape with 5 sides
		H. lose

34

Root Word, Prefix, & Suffix
Warm-ups: Final Review

Name/Date _____

Final Review 6

Write the words from the list to match the definitions.

closeness	darkness	disable
discolored	likeness	sickness

_____ poor health

_____ nearness

_____ similarity

_____ to put out of action

_____ stained

_____ lack of light

Name/Date _____

Final Review 7

On the lines, add three different prefixes to the root words. Write the new words.

cover	lay	cooked
_____	_____	_____
_____	_____	_____
_____	_____	_____

Name/Date _____

Final Review 8

All answers are words with suffixes.

1. What two-word rhyme describes someone who puts ducks into boxes? a _____ packer

2. What two-word rhyme describes a large rock in winter? a _____ boulder

3. What two-word rhyme describes a talkative parrot? a _____ birdy

4. What two-word rhyme describes a happy parrot? a _____ polly

---

Name/Date _____

Final Review 9

Match the words and their definitions.

____ 1. bicycle
____ 2. bimonthly
____ 3. decathlon
____ 4. discontinue
____ 5. harmful
____ 6. hexagon
____ 7. observatory

A. risky
B. 10-sport Olympic event
C. a vehicle with 2 wheels
D. a place to watch the stars and planets
E. every 2 months
F. stop
G. a shape with 6 sides

Name/Date _____

Final Review 10

Write the letter of the correct answer on the line.

_____ 1. think again   A. inconsiderate   B. reconsider   C. considerable
_____ 2. to stop something A. unavailable   B. continue   C. discontinue
_____ 3. unchanged   A. altered   B. unaltered   C. alternate
_____ 4. unhelpful   A. cooperation   B. cooperative   C. uncooperative
_____ 5. unnoticeable   A. undetectable   B. detection   C. detective
_____ 6. unwanted   A. desirable   B. unbelievable   C. undesirable
_____ 7. without end   A. limited   B. unlimited   C. unnecessary

Root Word, Prefix, & Suffix
Warm-ups: Final Review

Name/Date _____

Final Review 11

Match the words with their definitions.

_____ 1. biweekly   A. unsure

_____ 2. boastful   B. a 100-year celebration

_____ 3. centennial   C. every 2 weeks

_____ 4. cheerful   D. a group of things

_____ 5. combination   E. tasty

_____ 6. continuously   F. happy

_____ 7. doubtful   G. proud

_____ 8. flavorful   H. nonstop

Name/Date _____

Final Review 12

Add three different suffixes to the root words. Write the new words.

DISAGREEABLE

agree	bold	like
_____	_____	_____
_____	_____	_____
_____	_____	_____

Name/Date _____

Final Review 13

Write the words from the list to match the definitions.

bisect   **decorations**   **disadvantage**   **discharge**   **fanciful**   **millennium**
misdeed   **misshapen**   **mistreat**   **misuse**   **nonsense**   **observation**

_____ waste   _____ difficulty   _____ twisted

_____ set free   _____ harm   _____ foolishness

_____ crime   _____ 1,000 years   _____ ornaments

_____ imaginative   _____ cut in half   _____ close study

Name/Date _____

Final Review 14

Adding suffixes changes the part of speech of words. Write "N" if the word is a noun, "AV" if it is an adverb, or "AJ" if it is an adjective.

_____ 1. even   _____ 2. firm   _____ 3. lone

_____ 4. firmly   _____ 5. kindly   _____ 6. lazily

_____ 7. evenness   _____ 8. loneliness

_____ 9. kindness   _____ 10. laziness

Name/Date _____

Final Review 15

Match the words with their definitions.

_____ 1. triceratops   A. a 200-year celebration

_____ 2. octagon   B. a period of 10 years

_____ 3. octopus   C. the process of learning

_____ 4. decade   D. a shape with 8 sides

_____ 5. dutiful   E. an animal with 8 arms

_____ 6. education   F. obedient

_____ 7. bicentennial   G. a dinosaur with 3 horns

Words With Prefixes and/or Suffixes Used in This Book

acceptable	bluish	decline	dreadful	heliophobia	ingrown
accomplishment	boldness	decoration	drier	helpless	inhale
acrophobia	botanist	deduce	dutiful	hemicycle	inhuman
action	botany	deduct	easiness	hemisphere	inside
adaptable	broadly	deflate	education	hexagon	inspiration
adjustment	busier	deformed	Egyptian	higher	inspire
admiration	capitalization	dehumidifier	endless	honesty	interchange
adoption	careful	delay	equipment	hopeful	intercom
adoration	careless	demerit	evenness	horseless	intercontinental
advertisement	centennial	dentist	exception	hotter	interlocking
affordable	centimeter	depart	excite	hydrophobia	intermural
agreement	centipede	deport	excitement	hyperactive	Internet
alteration	centurion	descend	exfoliate	hypersensitive	interplanetary
alternate	century	desirable	exhale	hypersonic	interstate
alternately	charitable	detection	expiration	hypoactive	intramural
alternative	cheerful	detective	expire	hypothermia	intrastate
amazement	chemist	detector	export	ichthyology	investigate
amusement	chewable	dethrone	extrasensory	iciest	investigation
annoyance	childish	direction	fairness	illegal	investigator
anthropology	clarification	directive	faithful	illogic	investor
apiphobia	closeness	directly	fashionable	illogical	invitation
archaeology	closest	director	favorable	imagination	Irish
artist	colder	directory	fearless	immovable	Italian
assignment	colorful	disable	fiercely	impart	jolliest
Australian	colorless	disadvantage	Finnish	impatient	joyous
avoidable	combination	disagree	firmly	import	kindly
awareness	comfortable	disagreement	firmness	impossible	kindness
babyish	comparable	disappear	flier	impractical	laziness
baker	considerable	disapprove	florist	improbable	likable
bearable	consideration	disarm	freshest	improper	likely
beatable	contraction	discharge	friendless	inaction	likeness
beautification	cooperation	discolor	funnier	inactive	loneliness
beautiful	cooperative	disconnect	geology	inappropriate	loudly
bendable	cooperatively	disconnection	gladly	incapable	lovable
biannual	creation	discontinue	golfer	incite	macrocosm
bicentennial	cyclist	dislike	government	incompetent	macromolecule
bicycle	daily	disloyal	governor	inconsiderate	management
biennial	darkness	disobey	graceful	independent	meekness
bifocals	deactivate	disorder	graceless	indirect	megabytes
bilingual	deafness	displace	gratefully	indispensable	megaphone
bimonthly	debatable	disrepair	greenish	inequality	megasaurus
biologist	debug	disrespect	handful	infinite	meteorologist
biology	decade	disrespectful	happily	inflatable	Mexican
bisect	decagon	distrust	harmful	inflate	microcosm
biweekly	decathlon	dizziness	harpist	informal	Micronesia
blindness	December	donation	Hawaiian	informed	microphone

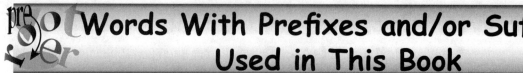

Words With Prefixes and/or Suffixes Used in This Book

microscope	overcoat	reconsider	submerge	undergraduate
millennium	overcooked	redder	subsoil	underground
milliliter	overdo	reddish	subtotal	underhanded
millimeter	overestimate	reduction	subtraction	underline
millipede	overflow	regulation	subtropical	underpaid
misbehave	overjoyed	reinvest	subway	underpass
misdeed	overpass	relay	Swedish	underpay
misfile	overpay	removable	tasteful	undersea
mislay	overtime	remove	tasteless	undersecretary
mislead	passable	repay	tastier	undertake
mismanagement	payable	replace	taxable	undesirable
mismatched	payment	report	tearful	undetectable
misshapen	pentagon	resell	therapist	undo
mistreat	pentathlon	reset	timidly	uneven
mistype	phobophobia	respectable	tiniest	unfair
misuse	pianist	restyle	treatment	unfamiliar
movable	playful	retry	triangle	unfed
mythology	plentiful	Roman	tricentennial	unfit
nearness	Polish	rudely	triceratops	unfriendly
neatly	politely	runner	tricycle	unglue
nervously	postgame	Russian	trilogy	unhappily
noisily	postnatal	sadder	triplets	unicorn
noncompliance	postoperative	sadly	tripod	unknown
nondairy	preassembled	semicircle	Turkish	unlike
nonfiction	predate	semicolon	twitching	unlikely
nonhuman	pregame	semifinal	typist	unlimited
nonobservance	prehistoric	semiprivate	unable	unlucky
nonpayment	preregister	semisweet	unaltered	unmade
nonprofit	preview	senseless	unbearable	unpaid
nonsense	proposal	sensor	unbelievable	unreal
nonstop	proposition	September	unbend	unset
nontoxic	psychology	shortly	unbolt	unstoppable
November	quadrilateral	shyly	unborn	unthinkable
observance	quadruplets	sickness	uncap	untie
observant	quicker	silently	unclear	untrue
observation	quickly	singer	unclog	unused
observatory	quickness	slowly	unconscious	unusual
observer	quietly	smartly	uncooperative	usable
octogenarian	quintet	Spanish	uncover	watcher
octagon	rarely	speediest	underage	weakly
October	reappearance	spiciest	underarm	wettest
octopus	reappoint	stylish	underclassman	wisest
older	reassure	subcommittee	undercooked	workable
oldest	recap	subdivide	underdeveloped	writer
overboard	rechargeable	subheading	underdog	zoology
overcharge	reconnect	submarine	underestimate	

38

Answer Keys

**Root Words, Prefixes, & Suffixes
1 (p. 2)**
Answers will vary.

**Root Words, Prefixes, & Suffixes
2 (p. 2)**
1. Answers will vary.
2. because the *re-* is part of the
   root word

**Root Words, Prefixes, & Suffixes
3 (p. 2)**
1. think   2. legal
3. honest   4. manage
5. possible   6. connect

**Root Words, Prefixes, & Suffixes
4 (p. 2)**
Answers will vary.

**Root Words, Prefixes, & Suffixes
5 (p. 2)**
Compound words are two or more
root words put together. Words with
prefixes and/or suffixes have one
root word with word parts added
to the beginning and/or end of the
word.

**Root Words, Prefixes, & Suffixes
6 (p. 3)**
1. believe   2. happy
3. appear   4. friend
5. charge   6. agree

**Root Words, Prefixes, & Suffixes
7 (p. 3)**
to do again

**Root Words, Prefixes, & Suffixes
8 (p. 3)**
Sentences will vary.
1. remove   2. repay
3. replace   4. reset
5. retry

**Root Words, Prefixes, & Suffixes
9 (p. 3)**
Definitions will vary.
1. reappoint   2. reconnect
3. redecorate   4. recheck
5. restyle

**Root Words, Prefixes, & Suffixes
10 (p. 3)**
Answers will vary.

**Prefixes With Negative Meanings
1 (p. 4)**
1. unlike   2. illogic
3. inappropriate 4. inconsiderate
5. nonprofit   6. disappear
7. disadvantage   8. nonsense
9. improbable   10. impossible

**Prefixes With Negative Meanings
2 (p. 4)**
They all mean "no" or "not."

**Prefixes With Negative Meanings
3 (p. 4)**
Definitions will vary.
1. unable   2. unlike
3. undo   4. unmade
5. uncover

**Prefixes With Negative Meanings
4 (p. 4)**
Answers will vary.

**Prefixes With Negative Meanings
5 (p. 4)**
1. disrepair   2. disarm
3. disorder   4. disloyal
5. disable   6. discolored
7. discharge   8. disrespect

**Prefixes With Negative Meanings
6 (p. 5)**
Answers will vary.

**Prefixes With Negative Meanings
7 (p. 5)**
1. distrust   2. disagree
3. untrue   4. displace
5. disobey   6. unbearable

**Prefixes With Negative Meanings
8 (p. 5)**
1. unlimited; without end
2. wrong; incorrect; unsuitable
3. restless; anxious
4. essential; vital
5. unreasonable; senseless

**Prefixes With Negative Meanings
9 (p. 5)**
unbend   unbolt   unborn
unclog   uneven   unfair
unfed   unfit   unglue
unknown   unmade   unreal
untied   untrue   unused
unusual

```
L N U L U U D E S U N U
A W U U A R N U U N N E
N O D U I X N R O B N U
S N E A V U R T E O U L
U K K E U N U N C L O G
N N N I N U D U N T U N
U U U N T I E D A M N U
```

**Prefixes With Negative Meanings
10 (p. 5)**
1. B   2. A   3. A
4. B   5. B

**Prefixes With Negative Meanings
11 (p. 6)**
1. impractical   2. insincere
3. informal   4. immovable
5. inappropriate 6. incapable
7. inequality   8. impossible
9. inflexible   10. improper

**Prefixes With Negative Meanings
12 (p. 6)**
Sentences will vary.
1. disadvantage   2. disapprove
3. disconnect   4. discontinue
5. disprove   6. dislike

**Prefixes With Negative Meanings
13 (p. 6)**
1. to not obey
2. Answers will vary. Any charity, etc.
3. not poisonous
4–5. Answers will vary.

39

Prefixes With Negative Meanings 14 (p. 6)
Answers will vary.

Prefixes With Negative Meanings 15 (p. 6)
1. E   2. D   3. F
4. B   5. A   6. C

Prefixes With Negative Meanings 16 (p. 7)
1. B   2. B   3. A
4. B   5. A   6. B

Prefixes With Negative Meanings 17 (p. 7)
1. e   2. f   3. a
4. b   5. d   6. c

Prefixes With Negative Meanings 18 (p. 7)
Answers will vary.

Prefixes With Negative Meanings 19 (p.7)
1. P: inactive   2. P: inaction
3. P: independent 4. C: into
5. P: ingrown   6. C: inchworm
7. P: inside   8. C: innkeeper

Prefixes With Negative Meanings 20 (p. 7)
Answers will vary.

Prefixes With Negative Meanings 21 (p. 8)
Answers will vary.

Prefixes With Negative Meanings 22 (p. 8)
1. *Nonstop* is something done or made without a stop or without letting up. *Unstoppable* is something that cannot be stopped.
2. *Nonhuman* is something that is not human. *Inhuman* means lacking pity or kindness; being cold or impersonal.
3. *Nonpayment* is a noun that usually refers to a bill that has not been paid. *Unpaid* is an adjective that means "not paid."

Prefixes With Negative Meanings 23 (p. 8)
1. The word is typed incorrectly.
2. The socks are not a pair; each one is different.
3. You could get lost.
4. Answers will vary. The student could be punished, etc.
5. It will be difficult to find the item when it is needed.

Prefixes With Negative Meanings 24 (p. 8)
Answers will vary.

Prefixes With Negative Meanings 25 (p. 8)
1. misshapen: twisted
2. mistreat: harm
3. nonsense: foolishness
4. nonfiction: truth
5. nonstop: continuously
6. misuse: waste

Prefixes Denoting Numbers 1 (p. 9)
Answers will vary.

Prefixes Denoting Numbers 2 (p. 9)
1. hexagon   2. triceratops
3. octopus   4. centennial

Prefixes Denoting Numbers 3 (p. 9)
1. decathlon   2. quadruplets
3. quintet   4. bimonthly

Prefixes Denoting Numbers 4 (p. 9)
1. 10   2. meter   3. 1,000
4. meter 5. 100   6. 1,000

Prefixes Denoting Numbers 5 (p. 9)
1. bilingual   2. pentathlon
3. bicentennial 4. trilogy
5. bisect   6. triplets
7. October

Prefixes Denoting Numbers 6 (p. 10)
1. July   2. November 2007
3. July 2005
4. Once every 100 years
5. July 4, 2076

Prefixes Denoting Numbers 7 (p. 10)
1. F   2. E   3. C
4. A   5. D   6. B

Prefixes Denoting Numbers 8 (p. 10)
1. millipede
2. 1,000   3. 100
4. Each lens is divided into two parts.

Prefixes Denoting Numbers 9 (p. 10)
Answers will vary.

Prefixes Denoting Numbers 10 (p. 10)
1 uni-   2 bi-   3 tri-
4 quad-   5 penta- or quin-
6 hex-   8 oct-   10 dec-
100 cent-   1,000 milli-

Prefixes *over-* and *under-* 1 (p. 11)
1. A   2. A   3. B   4. C
5. B   6. A   7. C   8. A
9. C   10. A 11. B 12. C

Prefixes *over-* and *under-* 2 (p. 11)
1. Answers will vary.
2. dishonest
3. They are not expected to win.
4. You are going to set out to do it; you take it upon yourself to do it.

Prefixes *over-* and *under-* 3 (p. 11)
Answers will vary.

Prefixes *over-* and *under-* 4 (p. 11)
1. work more than your regularly scheduled time
2. falls over the side of a boat or ship
3. not good; You have been charged too much.
4. You strain muscles, get tired, etc.
5. The water flows over the sides of the tub.

Prefixes *over-* and *under-* 5 (p. 11)
1. An *overpass* is the upper level of the crossing of a highway and another road or railroad. An *underpass* is the lower level of such a crossing.
2. To *overpay* is to pay too much. To *underpay* is to not pay enough.
3. underestimate

Prefixes 1 (p. 12)
1. to breathe out
2. to leave out
3. to burst outward
4. out

Prefixes 2 (p. 12)
1. To *incite* is to move to action or to urge on. To *excite* is to increase the activity of or stimulate.
2. *Import* is to bring something in. *Export* is to send something out.
3. *Expire* is to die, come to an end, or breathe one's last breath. *Inspire* is to motivate, affect, or breathe in.

Prefixes 3 (p. 12)
Answers will vary.

Prefixes 4 (p. 12)
1. small
2. a small community seen as representing the epitome, or best, of a larger community
3. it enlarges images of tiny objects so they can be seen

Prefixes 5 (p. 12)
1. semiprivate 2. exchange
3. semiprofessional
4. microscope 5. microphone
6. semicircle 7. hemisphere
8. semicolon 9. export
10. semisweet 11. semifinal
12. semiconscious
13. macromolecule
14. exfoliate 15. hemicycle

Prefixes 6 (p. 13)
1. EVA stands for extravehicular activity.
2. ESP stands for extrasensory perception.
3. ET stands for extraterrestrial.

Prefixes 7 (p. 13)
1. hyper- 2. hypo-
3. very loud 4. low

Prefixes 8 (p. 13)
submarine A subtropical C
subsoil A subway A
subcommittee B subdivide A
subheading A/B subtotal A

Prefixes 9 (p. 13)
1. Florida 2. smaller
3. smaller 4. larger
5. a lower layer

Prefixes 10 (p. 13)
1. ex- 2. hypo- 3. macro-
4. sub- 5. micro- 6. hyper-
7. semi- 8. extra- 9. hemi-

Prefixes 11 (p. 14)
1. interchange 2. intermural
3. intramural 4. interstate
5. intrastate
6. intercontinental

Prefixes 12 (p. 14)
Answers will vary.
3. IV means intravenous.

Prefixes 13 (p. 14)
1. pregame
2. A *preview* is a short part of a movie shown before the movie is available.
3. PS are words added after the closing of a letter. PS stands for *postscript*.
4. *pre-* means "before"
5. *post-* means "after"

Prefixes 14 (p. 14)
1. about 3 to 5 years old
2. No, postgraduate courses are taken after graduating from a four-year college.

3. Answers will vary.
4. before written history
5. Postnatal care is given after a baby is born.

Prefixes 15 (p. 14)
Answers will vary.

Prefixes 16 (p. 15)
1. megabats
2. 1,048,576 bytes in a megabyte (Accept one million.)
3. Answers will vary.

Prefixes 17 (p. 15)
Definitions will vary. Possible answers are given.
1. to pass from a higher place to a lower one
2. to remove insects; to eliminate errors
3. to put off, postpone
4. to infer from a general principle
5. to slope downward; to become less
6. a quality that deserves blame or lacks merit
7. to take away from a total

Prefixes 18 (p. 15)
Definitions may vary. Possible answers are given.
1. *Decline* is a downward slope or trend. *Incline* is an upward slope or trend.
2. To *increase* is to become progressively greater in size, number, etc. To *decrease* is to become less or reduced.
3. *Inflate* is to blow up or expand in size or importance. *Deflate* is to release air or reduce in size or importance.
4. To *deactivate* is to make inactive or ineffective. To *reactivate* is to make something active again or to revive.

Prefixes 19 (p. 15)
1. *Decline* is the process of falling, or going downhill, not the actual fall. *Decline* also has a prefix; *fall* does not.
2. dehumidifier
3. no

Prefixes 20 (p. 15)
The first three are false. The rest are true.

Prefixes 21 (p. 16)
1. no
2. Egyptian Empire
3. below
4. small

Prefixes 22 (p. 16)
Answers will vary.

Prefixes 23 (p. 16)
1. pre-
2. macro-
3. mis-
4. micro-
5. re-
6. over-
7. hyper-
8. sub-

Prefixes 24 (p. 16)
1. G
2. C
3. E
4. B
5. F
6. D
7. A

Prefixes 25 (p. 16)
Answers may vary. Possible answers are given.
1. deactivate
2. interstate, intrastate
3. deformed, preformed
4. preregister
5. depart
6. megaphone, microphone
7. deport, export
8. interactive, hyperactive, hypoactive

Prefix Review 1 (p. 17)
1. disagree
2. distrust
3. insincere
4. incorrect
5. indirect
6. immortal
7. impolite
8. misfit
9. mistrust
10. nonstop
11. nonprofit
12. overhead
13. overheat
14. overweight
15. unhappy
16. unselfish
17. underfoot
18. underline
19. replace
20. illegal

Prefix Review 2 (p. 17)
Answers will vary.

Prefix Review 3 (p. 17)
1. D
2. E
3. A
4. C
5. F
6. B

Prefix Review 4 (p. 17)
Sentences will vary.
1. unfamiliar
2. informal
3. illegible
4. impractical
5. dissatisfied, unsatisfied
6. intolerable

Prefix Review 5 (p. 17)
Definitions may vary. Possible answers given.
1. *Unable* means not capable of doing. *Disable* means to make incapable or ineffective.
2. *Mislay* means to misplace or lose something. To *relay* is to pass something along in stages.
3. *Nonstop* is something done without stopping. Something *unstoppable* cannot be stopped.
4. To *reset* is to set again or restart. *Unset* means something that is not set or fixed in place.
5. *Uncap* means to take off a cap or to open. *Recap* means to place a cap back on an opening or to close.
6. *Repaid* means to pay someone back. *Unpaid* means not paid.

Prefix Review 6 (p. 18)
1. no
2. no
3. yes
4. yes
5. yes
6. no
7. no
8. yes
9. yes
10. no
11. no
12. no

Prefix Review 7 (p. 18)
Definitions will vary. Possible answers are given.
1. To *miscalculate* is to calculate wrongly. To *recalculate* is to calculate again.
2. *Disorder* means out of order or in the wrong order. To *reorder* is to put back in order or to order something again.
3. *Bicentennial* is something that happens every 200 years. *Biannual* is something that happens twice a year.
4. *Removed* means that something has been moved or gotten rid of. *Unmoved* means that something has not been moved.
5. The *pentathlon* consists of five events. The *decathlon* consists of ten events.
6. *Quintuplets* are five of the same thing, usually babies born at the same time. *Quadruplets* are four of the same thing.

Prefix Review 8 (p. 18)
1. J
2. E
3. D
4. I
5. A
6. H
7. C
8. G
9. B
10. F

Prefix Review 9 (p. 18)
Answers may vary. Some possible answers are listed.
1. disloyal
2. biannual
3. discolor, recolor
4. bicycle, unicycle, tricycle, recycle
5. hemisphere
6. undone, redone, overdone, underdone
7. misuse, reuse
8. rethink
9. repaint
10. replace, displace, misplace

Prefix Review 10 (p. 18)
1. D
2. F
3. H
4. G
5. E
6. A
7. B
8. C

Prefix Review 11 (p. 19)
1. outside
2. huge
3. below
4. between
5. within
6. before
7. after
8. large
9. small
10. from or down

Prefix Review 12 (p. 19)
Answers will vary.

Prefix Review 13 (p. 19)
1. de(rail)   2. de(bug)
3. intra(mural)   4. inter(state)
5. sub(divide)   6. pre(existing)
7. de(merit)   8. post(game)
9. sub(way)   10. micro(scope)
11. mega(phone) 12. extra(ordinary)
13. mega(cycle) 14. de(port)
15. sub(marine)

Prefix Review 14 (p. 19)
Answers will vary.

Prefix Review 15 (p. 19)
1. megaorganisms
2. sell to
3. intracontinental
4. No
5. before written history
6. Answers will vary (any two planets).

Prefix Review 16 (p. 20)
1. T   2. T   3. F   4. F
5. F   6. T   7. T

Prefix Review 17–20 (p. 20)
Answers will vary.

Adding Suffixes 1–3 (p. 21)
Answers will vary.

Adding Suffixes 4 (p. 21)
The spelling of all words except *slow*, *tall*, *direct*, *rapid*, and *short* will change.

Adding Suffixes 5 (p. 21)
1. adopt   2. agree
3. style   4. combine
5. day   6. decorate
7. direct   8. govern
9. invite   10. twitch

Suffixes: -er, -or, -est 1 (p. 22)
1. hotter   2. sadder
3. colder   4. tastier
5. funnier   6. redder
7. higher   8. dryer *or* drier

Suffixes: -er, -or, -est 2 (p. 22)
Answers will vary.

Suffixes: -er, -or, -est 3 (p. 22)
1. speediest   2. wisest
3. closest   4. jolliest
5. tiniest   6. wettest
7. freshest   8. oldest
9. spiciest   10. yes
11. yes

Suffixes: -er, -or, -est 4 (p. 22)
1. baker   2. director
3. golfer   4. governor
5. jogger   6. singer
7. manager   8. writer

Suffixes: -er, -or, -est 5 (p. 22)
1. "one who"
2. Answers will vary.

Suffixes -ly and -ful 1 (p. 23)
1. neatly   2. slowly
3. fiercely   4. happily
5. gratefully 6. gladly
7. loudly   8. nervously
9. smartly   10. rarely
11. shortly   12. noisily

Suffixes -ly and -ful 2 (p. 23)
Sentences will vary. Adverb forms:
1. broadly   2. politely
3. quickly   4. quietly
5. rudely   6. sadly
7. shyly   8. silently
9. timidly   10. weakly

Suffixes -ly and -ful 3 (p. 23)
1. "filled with" or "full of"
2–3. Answers will vary.

Suffixes -ly and -ful 4 (p. 23)
1. colorful   2. faithful
3. graceful   4. hopeful
5. plentiful   6. playful

Suffixes -ly and -ful 5 (p. 23)
1. F   2. H   3. I   4. G
5. J   6. B   7. E   8. C
9. A   10. D

Suffixes -less, -tion, -ation 1 (p. 24)
1. *-less* means without or unable to act
2. Answers will vary.

Suffixes -less, -tion, -ation 2 (p. 24)
Some answers will vary.
1. tasteful   2. graceful
3. careful   4. eternal
5. no errors
6. There were no horses pulling them.

Suffixes -less, -tion, -ation 3 (p. 24)
Sentences will vary. Noun forms are:
1. donation   2. admiration
3. regulation 4. cooperation
5. inspiration

Suffixes -less, -tion, -ation 4 (p. 24)
1. act   2. adopt
3. except   4. direct
5. beauty   6. create
7. capital   8. subtract
9. reduce   10. clarify (clear)
11. contract   12. imagine

Suffixes -less, -tion, -ation 5 (p. 24)
1. I   2. B   3. J   4. H
5. C   6. F   7. E   8. D
9. A   10. G

Suffixes -able and -ment 1 (p. 25)
1. avoidable   2. bearable
3. beatable   4. bendable
5. comparable 6. correctable
7. inflatable 8. likable
9. lovable   10. removable
11. respectable 12. usable
13. capable of, fit for, or worthy of

Suffixes -able and -ment 2 (p. 25)
Answers will vary.

Suffixes -able and -ment 3 (p. 25)
Sentences will vary.
adaptable   comfortable
comparable   debatable
removable   desirable
favorable   chargeable
passable   respectable
(Note: chargeable is an exception to the spelling rule.)

Suffixes *-able* and *-ment* 4 (p. 25)
Definitions will vary.
adjustment   advertisement
amusement   assignment
excitement   judgment
(Note: judgment is an exception to the spelling rule.)
management   payment

Suffixes *-able* and *-ment* 5 (p. 25)
Answers will vary.

Suffixes *-ology, -ist, -phobia* 1 (p. 26)
1. life   2. animals
3. myths   4. the earth
5. people and cultures
6. the human mind
7. ancient artifacts and writings
8. fish

Suffixes *-ology, -ist, -phobia* 2 (p. 26)
1. plants   2. flowers
3. teeth   4. harp
5. biologist

Suffixes *-ology, -ist, -phobia* 3 (p. 26)
1. chemistry
2. bicycle, motorcycle, etc.
3. pianist
4. helps people overcome physical or mental problems through therapy
5. type
6. weather and climate

Suffixes *-ology, -ist, -phobia* 4 (p. 26)
1. heights   2. bees
3. water   4. sunshine
5. fear

Suffixes *-ology, -ist, -phobia* 5 (p. 26)
Answers will vary.

Suffixes *-ish, -ness, -an* 1 (p. 27)
Definitions will vary.
1. babyish   2. bluish
3. childish   4. greenish
5. reddish   6. stylish

Suffixes *-ish, -ness, -an* 2 (p. 27)
1. dizziness   2. easiness
3. firmness   4. laziness
5. loneliness   6. meekness

Suffixes *-ish, -ness, -an* 3 (p. 27)
1. meanness   2. boldness
3. numbness   4. fondness
5. likeness   6. darkness
7. closeness   8. awareness
9. deafness   10. quickness
11. sickness   12. blindness

Suffixes *-ish, -ness, -an* 4 (p. 27)
1. Swedish   2. Australian
3. Turkish   4. Finnish
5. Romans

Suffixes *-ish, -ness, -an* 5 (p. 27)
1. Spanish   2. Egyptian
3. Italian   4. Hawaiian
5. Russian   6. Polish
7. Mexican   8. Irish

Words With Prefixes & Suffixes 1 (p. 28)
1. direct   2. direct   3. direct
4. direct   5. invest   6. invest
7. invest   8. invest
9. observe   10. observe
11. observe   12. observe
13. propose   14. propose
15. invest

Words With Prefixes & Suffixes 2 (p. 28)
Answers will vary.

Words With Prefixes & Suffixes 3 (p. 28)
1. (n.) the act or process of changing; a change or modification
2. (adj.) every other one;
   (v.) to perform by turns;
   (n.) a substitute
3. (adv.) done in turns
4. (adj.) offering or expressing a choice; different from the usual;
   (n.) one of two or more choices
5. (adj.) not changed

Words With Prefixes & Suffixes 4 (p. 28)
Answers will vary.

Words With Prefixes & Suffixes 5 (p. 28)
Answers will vary. Some possible answers are fulfill, refill, filling, filler, fulfillment, overfill, unfilled, and unfulfilled.

Words With Prefixes & Suffixes 6 (p. 29)
Answers will vary.

Words With Prefixes & Suffixes 7 (p. 29)
1. (n.) something that serves to guide or direct;
   (adj.) intending to guide or direct
2. (adv.) in a direct manner; immediately; in a little while
3. (n.) one who directs
4. (n.) a wrong direction or the act of directing wrongly
5. (adj.) not direct or straightforward

Words With Prefixes & Suffixes 8 (p. 29)
1. B   2. C   3. C
4. A   5. B   6. C
7. A

Words With Prefixes & Suffixes 9 (p. 29)
1. N   2. N   3. A   4. A
5. A   6. V   7. N   8. V
9. N   10. V

Words With Prefixes & Suffixes 10 (p. 29)
Answers will vary. Possible answers include chargeable, uncharged, overcharged, undercharged, recharged, discharge, and turbocharger.

Words With Prefixes & Suffixes 11–12 (p. 30)
Answers will vary.

Words With Prefixes & Suffixes 13 (p. 30)
1. V/A 2. N   3. V   4. V
5. N   6. N   7. N   8. V
9. A   10. V

Words With Prefixes & Suffixes 14 (p. 30)
Answers will vary. Possible answers include friendly, unfriendly, friendless, befriend, friendship, unfriendliness, and friendliness.

Words With Prefixes & Suffixes 15 (p. 30)
1. F   2. T   3. F
4. T   5. T   6. T
7. F   8. T   9. T
10. F

Words With Prefixes & Suffixes 16 (p. 31)
1. B   2. E   3. A
4. F   5. D   6. C

Words With Prefixes & Suffixes 17 (p. 31)
1. (n.) the act of finding out
2. (n.) one who finds out or detects
3. (n.) one who detects or a device for detecting
4. (adj.) not able to be detected

Words With Prefixes & Suffixes 18 (p. 31)
1. V   2. N   3. N   4. N
5. N   6. N   7. V   8. N
9. A   10. A

Words With Prefixes & Suffixes 19 (p. 31)
Answers will vary. Possible answers include lovable, unloved, lovelier, lovely, loveliest, loving, lover, beloved, and loveless.

Words With Prefixes & Suffixes 20 (p. 31)
Answers will vary.

Suffix Review 1 (p. 32)
1. yes: beautiful
2. yes: desirable
3. no
4. no
5. yes: happily
6. yes: iciest

Suffix Review 2 (p. 32)
Answers will vary.

Suffix Review 3 (p. 32)

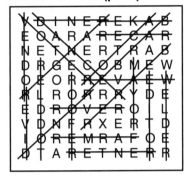

Suffix Review 4 (p. 32)
Answers will vary.

Suffix Review 5 (p. 32)
1. T   2. T
3. T   4. F
5. F   6. T

Suffix Review 6 (p. 33)
1. -ly   2. -able
3. -ish   4. -phobia
5. -ful   6. -less
7. -er   8. -ology

Suffix Review 7 (p. 33)
Examples will vary.
1. noun
3. adjective
5. adjective

Suffix Review 8 (p. 33)
1. no
2. yes: movable
3. yes: penniless
4. no
5. yes: sensor
6. yes: stylish

Suffix Review 9 (p. 33)
Examples will vary.
1. adverb
3. noun
5. noun

Suffix Review 10 (p. 33)
Answers will vary. Possible words include repay, prepay, payment, payable, paying, repayment, prepayment.

Final Review 1–2 (p. 34)
Answers will vary.

Final Review 3 (p. 34)
1. B   2. B
3. C   4. B
5. C   6. A
7. C

Final Review 4 (p. 34)
justice: fairness
daring: boldness
speed: quickness
rude: disrespectful
chaos: disorder
falling apart: disrepair

Final Review 5 (p. 34)
1. E   2. D
3. H   4. B
5. F   6. G
7. C   8. A

Final Review 6 (p. 35)
poor health: sickness
to put out of action: disable
nearness: closeness
stained: discolored
similarity: likeness
lack of light: darkness

Final Review 7 (p. 35)
Answers will vary. Some possible answers are listed.
cover: uncover, recover, undercover, discover
lay: underlay, overlay, relay, delay
cooked: uncooked, overcooked, undercooked, precooked

Final Review 8 (p. 35)
1. quacker
2. colder
3. wordy
4. jolly

Final Review 9 (p. 35)
1. C   2. E
3. B   4. F
5. A   6. G
7. D

Final Review 10 (p. 35)
1. B   2. C
3. B   4. C
5. A   6. C
7. B

Final Review 11 (p. 36)
1. C   2. G
3. B   4. F
5. D   6. H
7. A   8. E

Final Review 12 (p. 36)
Answer may vary. Some possible answers are listed.
agree: agreeable, agreement, agreeing, agreeably
bold: boldly, bolder, boldest, boldness
like: likely, likeness, likeliness, likelihood, likable

Final Review 13 (p. 36)
waste: misuse
difficulty: disadvantage
twisted: misshapen
set free: discharge
harm: mistreat
foolishness: nonsense
crime: misdeed
1,000 years: millennium
ornaments: decorations
imaginative: fanciful
cut in half: bisect
close study: observation

Final Review 14 (p. 36)
1. AJ
2. AJ or N
3. AJ
4. AV
5. AV or AJ
6. AV
7. N
8. N
9. N
10. N

Final Review 15 (p. 36)
1. G   2. D
3. E   4. B
5. F   6. C
7. A